Synthetic Phonics and Literacy Learning

An evidence-based critique

Margaret M Clark OBE

Glendale Education Birmingham

First edition published 2014

by Glendale Education: 61 Jacoby Place, Priory Road, Birmingham, B5 7UW

ISBN 978-0-9928931-1-8 (paperback)

ISBN 978-0-9928931-2-5 (ebook)

Printed in England and distributed by Witley Press Ltd, 24-26 Greevegate, Hunstanton, Norfolk, PE36 6AD
www.witleypress.co.uk

Contents

Preface

Over the years since 2006, synthetic phonics has become *the* required method of teaching reading in primary schools in England, and that to be emphasized by those training primary teachers. Since 2012 a phonics check has been administered to all children in year 1 (aged five and a half to six and a half years of age) and again in year 2 to any who fail to reach the pass mark. The focus in this book is the impact of *politics* on literacy policy, on the teaching and assessment of reading in early education in England, drawing on evidence from the imposition of synthetic phonics and the phonics check. The research base claimed for current policy is evaluated and its effects on practice in schools and some of the associated costs are explored. The findings from the interim reports of the government funded three-year research by the National Foundation for Educational Research are considered. The debate is widened to include evidence from other countries on the impact of commercialism on the literacy policies adopted by politicians. Questions are raised as to whose evidence should count in determining literacy policies.

This short publication brings together into a paperback and an ebook the information I have gathered over recent years on the issue of synthetic phonics as the best method of teaching reading. Edited versions of some of the information, initially published in the *Education Journal* in 2006-14, formed Section IV in *Learning to be Literate: insights from research for policy and practice* (Clark, M. M. 2014). Further information that appeared too late to be included in that book appeared in the *Education Journal* in May and September 2014. This material has been reorganised and edited to form an evidence-based critique on the effect of a policy of synthetic phonics as the required method of teaching reading in England over the past few years

Features of written English
There are twelve words on the outside cover:
Four are from the 100 key words in written English
Four are pseudo words from the 2014 Phonics Check
Four are words pronounced differently depending on the context

Acknowledgements

I am grateful to all these people, too many to name, friends and colleagues who have encouraged me throughout this new adventure into self-publishing. I could not have succeeded in bringing this to fruition without the assistance and technical ability of the following:

Bob Ridge-Stearn, Head of e-Learning at Newman University and Samantha Bryant, for their crucial technical support and patience with my naïve questions;

Demitri Coryton, editor of the *Education Journal*, for publishing my articles and permitting me to adapt them for this book;

Chris Witley, of Witley Press Ltd, for his speedy response to my many queries and his company's efficient treatment of my work.

While this new venture has on occasion been stressful, it has also been a challenge, and fun. Furthermore, I can now claim not only to have had this book printed speedily, to my specifications, but also to be a publisher!

Margaret M Clark   2014

Chapter 1

Introduction

Rationale for the book

There still seems to be insufficient acknowledgement of the wide differences between children on entry to school in their concepts of print, even where none can yet read, or of the needs of children who enter school already reading silently and with understanding. Over a long career I have undertaken research into a wide range of issues in education, where I felt greater insight was needed. One such current issue seems to me to be the imposition of one method, claimed to be *the* method of teaching reading, namely synthetic phonics, first fast and only. I have watched claims made for specific approaches to teaching reading, each claimed to be a panacea. In 1960s it was The Initial Teaching Alphabet (ita), currently it is synthetic phonics.

Should we be concerned that for the past three years all children around six years of age in England have been expected to pass a test of reading aloud 40 words, half of which are 'pseudo' words, such as vol, teg, ind, tull, shog? Should they fail to reach the expected level they are required to re-sit the test the following year. This test must be sat even by children who can already read and by children for whom English is not their mother tongue. Rather than a 'light touch' diagnostic assessment this has become a high stakes test. Many schools anxious to achieve the required high percentage pass rate have been purchasing commercial materials and practising for the test, including pseudo words.

What would you believe are the critical features of written English based on such experiences?

Hopefully the evidence presented here might put to rest some myths, including those perpetuated by successive governments, where they fly in the face of a wealth of research evidence.

Outline of the book

The focus here is on the influence of politics on policy and practice, following claims made by the Coalition Government in 2010 that there is one best method for teaching reading, namely synthetic phonics and the demand that this be adopted in all primary schools in England. The phonics check of 40 words, 20 pseudo words and 20 real words, to be read aloud, was introduced in 2012. This is required to be taken by all children in State schools in England at the end of year 1, and re-taken the following year by any child who fails to achieve the pass mark. This has become a high stakes test with percentage pass being recorded for individual schools and subgroups within schools, with monitoring over the years of the increasing percentage of children passing the test. This improvement in percentage pass, attributed by the government to the introduction of synthetic phonics and the check, is claimed as showing improvement in reading. This data is available online to Ofsted, where an important aspect of their inspection is a check on the implementation of this government policy. This is true both in schools, and for those training teachers, who are required to give high priority to this in their courses.

I have been able to study not only the results of the check over the first three years of its imposition, but also relevant information from other sources. The claims for synthetic phonics can be traced back in England to the Rose Report in 2006. My critique of The Rose Report, which paved the way for the recent emphasis on synthetic phonics first fast and only as *the* method of teaching reading, is reprinted as chapter 13 in *Learning to be Literate* (Clark, 2014). It is briefly summarised here in chapter 2. The evidence that there is one best method of teaching reading for all children and that it is synthetic phonics (as opposed to analytic phonics) is considered in chapter 3, analysing both evidence cited by the government and conflicting evidence. I have drawn on a wide range of research from 1960s to the present day, revealing little evidence for one best method of teaching reading, and certainly not for the superiority of synthetic phonics as *the* method as opposed to analytic phonics.

Phonics instruction refers to literacy teaching approaches that focus on the relationship between letters and sounds. Most would not dispute that for most children there may be a need for *systematic* teaching of phonics, but within a broad programme. The debate considered here is as to whether phonics should be the only method employed in the early stages, the books on which the children are learning should be confined to simple texts, and whether synthetic phonics instruction is superior to analytic phonics. The defining characteristics of synthetic phonics are sounding out and blending. Analytic phonics avoids sounding out, inferring sound-symbol relationships from sets of words.

The phonics check has been administered to all children at the end of year 1, aged from five and a half to six and a half years of age, since 2012, and retaken by any child the following year who failed to achieve the pass mark of 32 out of 40 words correctly read aloud. Its development, results and effects after the first and second years of its administration, 2012 and 2013, are discussed in chapter 4. In 2014 there was a change in administration, where the pass mark was not divulged in advance, but was in fact the same as in the two preceding years. In chapter 5 the implications of this change, the results for 2014 compared to the two previous years, and the claims made for improvement in standards of reading attributed by the government, and reported uncritically in most of the media are considered.

In chapter 6 some of the costs of the phonics check and of the commercial materials and training courses recommended by the government and available through a match-funding scheme are discussed. This information was obtained under the Freedom of Information Act. In the second part of that chapter the discussion is widened with evidence from a recently published book, *Whose Knowledge Counts in Government Literacy Policies?* K. S. Goodman, R. C. Calfee and Y. M. Goodman (eds) (2014). It appears that commercial interests are gaining an increasingly powerful place in government policies in many parts of the world, including, The United States, Germany, France and also in many developing countries. The theme has now become 'Whose Knowledge Counts in Literacy Policies?' A disquieting picture is painted of the power wielded by large commercial organisations to influence government literacy policies, often falsely claiming a research basis for the policy.

A three-year research has been funded by DfE and the results of the two interim reports from the National Foundation for Educational Research are available and are discussed in chapters 7. The final report is not due until around May 2015, about the time of the General Election. In the interim reports NFER has already raised a number of important issues about the validity of the scores and the understanding of many teachers of the distinction between synthetic phonics (that required) and analytic phonics. A summary of the claims by the government for the phonics check are also reported.

Government Policy in England on Learning to Read 2006 to 2014

The origins of the Coalition Government's policy in England for the teaching of reading can be traced back to the Rose Report in 2006, which under a Labour Government raised the issue of synthetic phonics as the way to teaching reading. A critique of that report is to be found in chapter 13 of *Learning to be Literate* (Clark, 2014, adapted from Clark 2006). This is summarized in the following chapter, chapter 2.

References

Clark, M. M. (2014) *Learning to be Literate: insights from research for policy and practice.* Birmingham: Glendale Education.

Goodman, K. S., Calfee, R.C. and Goodman, Y. M. (eds) (2014) *Whose Knowledge Counts in Government Literacy Policies? Why expertise matters.* New York: Routledge.

Chapter 2

The Rose Report and the Teaching of Reading

This is a shortened version of chapter 13 in *Learning to be Literate* (Clark, 2014).

The background

The Rose Report, published in 2006, was commissioned following an enquiry by a Select Committee of the House of Commons, and at the request of the Labour Government then in power. Its claims for synthetic phonics as the method for teaching beginning reading have had a major impact in schools and on the training of teachers in England, and become the basis for the Coalition Government's policy since 2010. Claims for synthetic phonics as the method of teaching reading pre date the edicts from the Coalition Government in England from 2010 discussed in the following chapters. In an article in the *Education Journal* (Issue 94 2006, 28) entitled, 'This could be the end of teacher autonomy', Colin Richards commented:

> 'Well in a few months time, teachers of young children could be required to teach initial reading through synthetic phonics – a method not dissimilar to those used in Victorian classrooms'.

One must wonder if his prediction has been realised?

The decision to establish the Rose inquiry was stimulated by the report of the all-party House of Commons Education and Skills Committee, *Teaching Children to Read* (April 2005). The publicity from the media and from politicians around that report had as its main focus phonics, more particularly synthetic phonics. Much of the oral evidence presented to the Committee was from proponents of synthetic phonics, several of them with a commercial interest in programmes for schools. Rhona Johnston was questioned on evidence from her research in primary schools in

Clackmannanshire, a small county in Scotland. Thereafter Clackmannanshire has frequently been cited in England, though few references identify the precise nature of this research. NB Nick Gibb, Minister of State at the DfE, when in Opposition, was a member of the Select Committee that predated the Rose Report. Since then, an advocate and strong supporter of synthetic phonics, still in 2014 he cites this study as the research evidence base for the coalition government's policy.

The Select Committee recommendations

It is worth reminding readers that the House of Commons Select Committee that led to the setting up of the Rose enquiry stressed that:

> Whatever method is used in the early stages of teaching children to read, we are convinced that inspiring an enduring enjoyment of reading should be a key objective. This can be endangered both by an overtly formal approach in the early years and by a failure to teach decoding. (36)

The Committee also recommended that an inquiry should be set up and evidence should be sought to establish among other points:

How long any gains from a particular programme are sustained; the effectiveness of different approaches with particular groups of children, including boys/girls, those with special educational needs and those with a high level of socio-economic disadvantage. (36)

No such research was funded.

Setting for the Rose Report

Following the report of the Select Committee, on 22 June 2005 the then Secretary of State for Education, Ruth Kelly, wrote to Jim Rose and in her letter, she set out three points she wished to be considered in his report:

- What our expectations of best practice should be in the teaching of early reading and synthetic phonics for primary schools and early years settings, including both the content and the pace of teaching.

- How this relates to the development of the birth-to-five framework and the ongoing development and renewal of the National Literacy Framework for teaching.
- What range of provision best supports children with significant literacy difficulties and enables them to catch up with their peers, and the relationship of such targeted intervention programmes with synthetic phonics teaching.

Following the interim report in December 2005 already Ruth Kelly was making it clear that she was fully in support of the report's recommendation that a systematic, direct teaching of synthetic phonics should be the first strategy taught to all children learning to read, introduced by the age of five.

The Rose Report

The Final Rose Report in March 2006 contained a wide range of recommendations designed to improve the teaching of reading. However, all the attention seems to have been focused on the synthetic phonics issue. This is not surprising in view of the statements by the Secretary of State who commissioned the report and the fact that already by page 3 the report states:

> Engaging young children in interesting and worthwhile pre-reading activities paves the way for the great majority to make a good start on systematic phonic work by the age of five. Indeed, for some, an earlier start may be possible and desirable.

Among the reactions to the interim report were concerns that the recommendations could be seen as claiming that one size fits all. Parents must have been concerned or confused at the mixed messages they were receiving from the media following the Rose Report about their role in their children's early learning to read. This at a time when research had shown just how much parents can and do contribute.

There was a lack of reference in the report to provision for young children who are already able to read with fluency and understanding when they enter school, also those children whose language difficulties may make a focus on phonics at too early an age a stumbling block to their learning. Not all reading specialists would agree with the following:

> An early start on systematic phonic work is especially important for those children who do not have the advantages of strong support for literacy at home. (31)

Critique of the Rose Report

Many young children entering school, even in 2006, were already more computer-literate than their teachers in this age of digital literacy. This deserves more attention than it received in the Rose Report. Why in the United Kingdom, in England in particular, is it considered to be progress to introduce children to reading, and especially phonics, so early and so long before the teaching of reading takes place in most other countries? This includes many countries with higher standards of literacy than England. Surely there is a case to be made for broadening the curriculum and for delaying the teaching of reading, particularly in a language such as English with its deep orthography, in contrast to other languages with a shallow orthography, such as Finnish, in which the relationship is coherent and consistent. See chapter 8 here, and 'Orthographies and Literacy' for more detail in *Learning to be Literate* (Clark, 2014: 215-16). A later start in formal instruction might make such instruction less time-consuming as a consequence of the children's greater maturity and better-developed listening skills.

Politicians and others gave the impression that an injection of synthetic phonics first, fast and only as soon as children enter school, would solve all reading problems. Some of the invective has been reminiscent of the hype that surrounded the introduction of ita (the initial teaching alphabet) over 50 years ago.

The Clackmannanshire Research

The Rose Committee did visit Clackmannanshire and several pages in the report are devoted to the approach to the teaching of literacy they found there, but there is no critical evaluation of the research (61-5). Frequent reference was made in the media to the 'spectacular' results from that research; these were only in the children's word recognition skills, rather than in their understanding. Criticisms of the methodology of the research have been voiced by a number of experts, including lack of attention to other aspects of the intervention programme (see chapter 3).

Comments

One must consider whether the research evidence on synthetic phonics was as strong as suggested in the Rose Report and justified the stance by the Coalition Government in 2010 that the teaching of reading should be through the use of synthetic phonics, first, fast and only; that a phonics check be administered to all children in year 1 whether or not they could already read; that half the words should be pseudo words and that pass/fail with an arbitrary score of 32 out of 40 should be the recorded evidence.

References

Clark, M. M. (2014) *Learning to be Literate: insights from research for policy and practice.* Birmingham: Glendale Education.

House of Commons (2005) *Teaching Children to Read.* Report of the Education and Skills Select Committee. London: The Stationery Office.

Kelly, R. (2005) Letter to Jim Rose from The Secretary of State. 22nd June.

Richards, C. (2006) 'This could be the end of teacher autonomy'. *Education Journal.* Issue 94: 19.

Rose, J. (2006) *Independent Review of the Teaching of Early Reading.* Final Report. www.standards.dfes.gov.uk/rosereview.

Chapter 3

One Best Method of Teaching Reading?

This chapter is based on chapter 14 in *Learning to be Literate* (Clark, 2014).

Background

As noted in the previous chapter, as early as 2005, during a Labour Government, claims were being made for the importance of synthetic phonics as an important element in the teaching of reading. This featured in evidence to the Education and Skills Select Committee (2005) and in 2006 in the subsequently commissioned Rose Report.

It is important to distinguish the following:

whether there evidence for one best method of teaching reading for all children;

whether systematic teaching of phonics should form all or at least part of children's early instruction;

whether this should be synthetic phonics rather than analytic phonics.

The coalition government in England, and Ofsted, have since 2010 stressed that the method of teaching reading should be phonics, and synthetic phonics, rather than analytic phonics, claiming this is backed by research evidence.

Definitions of phonics

Phonics instruction: Literacy teaching approaches which focus on the relationship between letters and sounds.

Systematic phonics instruction: Teaching of letter-sound relationships in an explicit, organised and sequential fashion as opposed to incidentally or on a 'when-needed' basis.

Synthetic phonics: The defining characteristics of synthetic phonics for reading are sounding-out and blending.

Analytic phonics: The defining characteristics of analytic phonics are avoiding sounding-out, and inferring sound-symbol relationships from sets of words.

(From Torgerson *et al* 2006: 8)

The evidence for one best method of teaching reading for all children will be considered, with quotations from a range of researchers, followed by an analysis of the evidence cited by the government, claimed to support synthetic phonics as the method to be used in all schools and emphasised in all courses training teachers. Finally research evidence not cited by the government will be introduced where the claims for synthetic phonics have been disputed.

Is there one best method?

As early as 1967 as shown by Jeanne Chall in *Learning to Read: the great debate*, there was extensive research and a longstanding debate about whether there was one best method of teaching reading and the controversies surrounding this. In 1972 Vera Southgate in *Beginning Reading*, commented:

> I think it is highly unlikely that one method or scheme will ever prove equally effective for all pupils, being taught by all teachers, in all situations. (28)

In the Bullock Report (*A Language for Life,* DES, 1975) it is stated that:

> There is no one method, medium, approach, device, or philosophy that holds the key to the process of learning to read. Too much

attention has been given to polarised opinions about approaches to the teaching of reading. (521)

The report from the House of Commons Select Committee (2005) referred to above states that it is 'unlikely that any one method or set of changes would lead to a complete elimination of underachievement of reading'. (3)

More recently, in July 2011 a House of Commons All Party Parliamentary Group for Education published its Report of the Inquiry into Overcoming the Barriers to Literacy, stating that:

> Respondents were clear that there is no one panacea which guarantees all children will become readers... There are different ways to learn and different learning preferences, this is why a focus on only synthetic phonics is not appropriate. (www.educationengland.org.uk: 14).

Marilyn Adams (1990) in *Beginning to Read: thinking and learning about print*, emphasises that:

> the degree to which children internalize and use their phonic instruction depends on the degree to which they have found it useful for recognizing the words in their earliest texts...immersion – right from the start – in meaningful connected text is of vital importance. (10)

The research evidence on synthetic phonics

Following the government's announcement in 2010, many experts wrote to DfE stating their concern about the insistence that in all schools in England the initial approach to teaching reading should be synthetic phonics only, also about the proposed phonics check for six-year-olds. *The Importance of Phonics: Securing Confident Reading* (www.education.gov.uk) cites researches such as several of those noted below claimed to prove the superiority of synthetic phonics as the only method for teaching reading. However, none of the researches cited below provide convincing evidence for synthetic phonics as the only approach in the early stages of learning to read.

In my critique of the Rose Report (2006) I noted that no reference was made there to the comprehensive research by Torgerson *et al* (2006) where it is claimed that there is evidence that *systematic teaching of phonics* benefits children's reading accuracy, it should be part of every literacy teacher's repertoire, in a judicious balance with other elements.

> No statistically significant difference in effectiveness was found between synthetic phonics instruction and analytic phonics instruction. (8)

I analysed the evidence cited in the Rose Report from the Clackmannanshire study which had methodological failings, and where there was little long term gain in reading comprehension (see summary in the previous chapter). This research and another from a Scottish local authority, West Dunbartonshire, are the researches frequently cited by the government in support of its current emphasis on synthetic phonics first, fast and only in the initial stages. However, they do not mention that in both these authorities this was part of a major intervention study with additional resources and a staff development programme (see Ellis, 2007). Sue Ellis in her article 'Policy and research: lessons from the Clackmannanshire synthetic phonics initiative', states that:

> any study driven mainly by one paradigm can only offer limited insights and that other Scottish local authorities deliberately created multi-paradigm projects in response to the national early intervention initiatives.

She also refers to the West Dunbartonshire research, claiming it as, 'possibly the most successful intervention, and based on a 'literacy for all' agenda' (294). In the final report of that research MacKay in 2007 provides an overview of the entire 10-year study. He cites the following as crucial to the success of the project:

phonological awareness and the alphabet; a strong and structured phonics emphasis; extra classroom help in the early years; raising teacher awareness; and home support for encouraging literacy through focused assessment; increased time spent on key aspects of reading; identification and support for children who are failing, and close monitoring of progress.

The project needed to be long term, have substantial funding and high levels of training of staff.

The coalition government in England cites this study as evidence for synthetic phonics, but omits to mention the above crucial elements of that research, and omits to note this final sentence in the paragraph they cite, as to whether synthetic phonics:

> has not yet been sufficiently systematically compared with better analytic phonics teaching using a faster pace and more motivating approaches. (46)

In a comprehensive research on real books versus reading schemes, Solity and Vousden (2009) analysed the structure of adult literature, children's real books, and reading schemes, and examined the demands they make on children's sight vocabulary and phonic skills. While they claim that learning phonic skills greatly reduces what children have to memorise, a combination of this and learning the 100 commonest sight words, and studying in the context of real books makes for 'optimal instruction'. Note that these authors used the McNally and Murray 100 commonest word list from 1960s in their analysis. They still found it valuable in 2009. The authors claim that:

> the debate may be resolved by teaching an optimal level of core phonological, phonic, and sight vocabulary skills, rigorously and systematically in conjunction with the use of real books. (503)

In chapter 9 of *Learning to be Literate* (Clark, 2014), based on a recent article on the use of high frequency words in helping children who are learning to read, I also used the McNally and Murray 100 key words.

In 2007, Wyse and Styles in an article entitled, 'Synthetic phonics and the teaching of reading: the debate surrounding England's Rose Report', review the international research into the teaching of early reading and claim that the Rose Report's main recommendation on synthetic phonics contradicts the powerful body of evidence accumulated over the last 30 years'. (35)

> The conclusion of the Rose Report, that teachers and trainee teachers should be required to teach reading through synthetic phonics 'first and fast' is, in our view, wrong. (41)

A further article in which the government's view is challenged is that by Wyse and Goswami (2008). They claim that the government's review provided no reliable empirical evidence that synthetic phonics offers the vast majority of beginners the best route to becoming skilled readers.... 'There is also evidence that contextualised systematic phonics instruction is effective'. (691)

In 2012, David Reedy having explored the evidence for the quotations from Nick Gibb, Schools Minister since 2010, challenges his claims, citing contradictory evidence from Ofsted.

Footnote

IMPACT pamphlet Number 20 by Andrew Davis, 'To read or not to read: decoding synthetic phonics', was launched at a symposium in The Institute of Education in London on 29 January 2014. The pamphlet was an extended version of an article in the *Journal of Philosophy of Education* in 2012, with the title, 'A monstrous regimen of synthetic phonics: fantasies of research based teaching 'methods' versus real teaching'. Davis argues his points powerfully, insisting that there is no justification for the universal imposition of any one teaching method, and of synthetic phonics in particular. He states that he is not opposed to phonics as such and that teachers should ensure that children learn the conventional letter sounds correspondence and that as appropriate they use such knowledge in early reading. However, he argues as have many others, that it should be suitably embedded in the context of reading for meaning' (6), and on page 7 goes on to state that if we sought to favour phonics at all we should support analytic phonics.

He expresses particular concern about the effect of this policy and the phonics check required of all 5 and 6-year-old children in England on children who can already read, referring to it as 'an abuse'. He also deplores the restriction in the type of reading material by which children may now be taught in the early stages. He argues (on page 14) that synthetic phonics, with its accompanying phonics check, at least in its pure form, fails to take account of the true character of reading and of the gulf between reading and decoding. Like others, he claims that there will inevitably be some teaching to the test with its high stakes. According to Davis, blending individual letters does not immediately result in words as such; in English for some words the reader must know the context to be able to pronounce the words. Davis' pamphlet was endorsed by Professor Sir Tim Brighouse, who was also a member of the panel at the launch. He endorsed it on the back cover:

> Here is a book which every primary school should have for its teachers… and if they take its lessons to heart, they will have the moral courage and the knowledge to back their own professional judgement and do what they think is right – which will not be to do as the government suggests.

At the symposium, Professor Brighouse, in his final comments widened the discussion beyond the pamphlet, to deplore the fact that in England now not only can the Secretary of State for Education tell teachers what to teach but how to teach. He worried should a medical consultant be expected to adopt a similar stance!

Conclusion

The researchers cited in this chapter support the belief that:

There is benefit from the inclusion of phonics within the early instruction in learning to read in English, within a broad programme.

There is *not* evidence to support phonics in isolation as the one best method.

There is *not* evidence for synthetic phonics as the required approach rather than analytic phonics.

References

Adams, M. J. (1990) *Beginning to Read: thinking and learning about print.* Cambridge, Mass: MIT.

Chall, J. (1967) *Learning to Read: the great debate.* New York: McGraw-Hill.

Clark, M. M. (2014) 'High frequency words: a neglected resource in learning to read'. Chapter 9 in *Learning to be Literate: insights from research for policy and practice.* Birmingham: Glendale Education.

Davis, A. (2014) 'To read or not to read: decoding synthetic phonics', *IMPACT* No.20. www.philosophy-of-education.org. Wiley.

DES (1975) *A Language for Life* (The Bullock Report). London: HMSO.

DfE (2010) The Importance of Phonics: securing confident reading. Online at www.education.gov.uk.

Ellis, S. (2007) 'Policy and research: lessons from the Clackmannanshire synthetic phonics initiative'. *Journal of Early Childhood Literacy.* Vol 7(3): 281-297.

House of Commons (2005) *Teaching Children to Read.* Report of the Education and Skills Select Committee. London: The Stationery Office.

House of Commons (1911) *Report of the Inquiry into Overcoming the Barriers to Literacy.* London: The Stationery Office.

MacKay, T. (2007) *Achieving the Vision.* The final report of the West Dunbartonshire Literacy Initiative. (Education.centralregistry@west-dunbarton.gov.uk).

Reedy, D. (2012) 'Misconceptions about teaching reading: is it only about phonics?' *Education Review.* NUT (EPC) vol. 24 (2).

Rose, J. (2006) *Independent Review of the Teaching of Early Reading.* Final Report. www.standards.dfes.gov.uk/rosereview.

Solity, J. and Vousden, J. (2009) 'Real books vs reading schemes: a new perspective from instructional psychology'. *Educational Psychology.* Vol 29 (4): 469-511.

Southgate, V. (1972) *Beginning Reading.* London: University of London Press.

Torgerson, C. J., Brooks, G. and Hall, J. (2006) *A Systematic Review of the Research Literature on the use of Phonics in the Teaching of Reading and Spelling.* Research report RR711 DfES online www.dfes.gov.uk/research.

Wyse, D. and Goswami, U. (2008) 'Synthetic phonics and the teaching of reading'. *British Educational Research Journal.* Vol 34 (6): 691-710.

Wyse, D. and Styles M (2007) 'Synthetic phonics and the teaching of reading: the debate surrounding England's Rose report'. *Literacy.* Vol. 41: 35-42.

NB. See chapter 6 here and *Whose Knowledge Counts in Government Literacy Policies? Why expertise matters*, (2014) K. S. Goodman, R. C. Calfee and Y. M. Goodman (eds). This publication widens the discussion to include other countries including USA, Germany and France.

Chapter 4

The Phonics Check: the initial results

Background

Over the years claims have been made for one best method of teaching reading, not necessarily the same method. These claims were analysed in the previous chapter. In England the coalition government has claimed that the one best method of teaching reading is by synthetic phonics, first, fast and only, with implications for schools, the curriculum and for the training of teachers. Synthetic phonics has as its focus the relationship between letters and sounds and differs from analytic phonics in that these features are taught in isolation rather than inferring sound-symbol relationships from sets of words. In June 2012 a phonics check of 40 words (20 pseudo words and 20 real words) was administered to all Year 1 children in state schools in England for the first time with children required to read the words out loud to a teacher. In June 2013 a similar test was administered to all Year 1 children, and to those who had failed to achieve the pass mark of 32 out of 40 the previous year. This has been repeated in 2014 with only a minor change in that the pass mark was not revealed in advance in 2014. Depending on which paper you read the results for the first two years showed either that two thirds of six-year-olds passed the tests by 2013, or that 'one in three six-year-olds in England struggle with reading' (*The Guardian*, 3.10.13).

In the 2010 White Paper *The Importance of Teaching* the DfE signalled its intent to introduce a Phonics Screening Check at the end of Year 1 (to five and six-year-old pupils) in all primary schools in England – designed to be 'a light touch, summative assessment'. The claim was that this would 'identify pupils with below expected progress in phonic decoding'. Such pupils were to receive intervention, and retake the test the following year. A pilot study across 300 schools was commissioned in 2011 (*Process*

Evaluation of the Year 1 Phonics Screening Pilot, 2012, www.shu.ac.uk/ceir), to help plan the administration of the check, not to decide whether it would be implemented.

Note the difference between *systematic teaching of phonics* and the use of either *synthetic* or *analytic* phonics as the actual method of teaching. The government documents emphasise synthetic phonics as the method to be used.

Initial concerns

Following the government's announcement in 2010, many experts wrote to DfE stating their concern about the insistence that in all schools the initial approach to teaching reading should be synthetic phonics only, and about the proposed phonics check. Following the first nationwide administration of the Check in June 2012, with a pass set at 32 out of 40, claimed to be the age appropriate level, further concerns were expressed at many aspects:

- the pass/fail decision resulting in many children aged between five and six years of age and their parents being told they have failed;
- the inclusion of 20 pseudo words in the test;
- the demand that the children who 'failed' retake the test the following year;
- the match-funding for schools to purchase commercial phonics materials and training courses for teachers on synthetic phonics (from a recommended list) with a monitoring of this by DfE;
- the lack of any diagnostic aspects or suggestion that other methods may be appropriate for some children who have failed;
- possible effects on some successful readers who may yet have failed this test.

According to a DfE press release, by January 2012 thousands of schools had already spent 'more than £7.7 million on new phonics products and training from a 'phonics catalogue of approved products and services''. Furthermore schools could claim up to £3000 to buy such products and training until

March 2013. Nick Gibb, the Schools Minister, invited schools to purchase such materials, 'to improve the way they teach systematic synthetic phonics - the tried and tested method of improving the reading of our children, especially the weakest'. He reprimanded local authorities where the uptake had been low, in spite of the fact that some schools might well have had adequate supplies of materials. The match-funding was extended to October 2013. See chapter 6 for further information on the costs of this match-funding.

The results of the first phonics check

The Statistical First Release of the results of the phonics screening test was published in September 2012.What was claimed as the 'expected standard of phonic decoding', namely 32 out of 40, was met by only 58% of pupils (62% of girls and 54% of boys). One must question the authority for this 'threshold'.

In the report there is a breakdown for different groups of children, showing wide variation in the pass rate:

- 62% of girls scored 32 or more but only 54% of boys;
- only 44% of those on free meals met this 'required standard';
- An even more striking finding is that, 'Travellers of Irish Heritage and those of a Gypsy/Roma background' were the groups with the lowest percentages achieving the required standard in phonics, 16 and 17 per cent respectively.

However, no tables were published of percentage pass rate by month of birth, in spite of the fact that there was a year's difference in age between the youngest and oldest children taking the check. I requested this information. A comparison by date of birth reveals striking differences between the oldest and youngest children. The pass rate for the oldest boys was 65% and for the youngest (still only five years of age) was 44%; for girls the two figures were 72% and 51%.

The teachers were informed in advance that 32 out of 40 was the pass mark, pass or fail being the only recorded information. A breakdown by percentages scoring each mark reveals that while only 2% of pupils gained a mark of 31, 7% were awarded 32. This pattern is unlikely to be explained by the structure of the test; it must have been tempting to give one more mark when that meant a pass! Not only were the parents of those who 'failed' informed, but the children were required to retake this test in 2013, having had further synthetic phonics instruction, with the schools 'encouraged' to purchase commercial programmes. One must question whether this is the appropriate action on the basis of these results.

Having seen the actual test I became even more disturbed. The first twelve words were all pseudo words, starting with pib, vus, yop, elt, desh. What message does this give to children about reading? There is evidence from the online surveys by UKLA and the teachers' unions that some of those confused by the pseudo words were children who were already reading.

Why spend money on developing such a pass/fail test, and why test all year 1 children (about 600,000) rather than extend the use of diagnostic tests such as Reading Recovery, providing as it does diagnostic information and proven intervention strategies with long term effects?

Effects on schools, the curriculum and teacher training

On schools: UKLA and teachers' unions (ATL/NAHT/NUT) investigated the views of teachers' on the phonics check. Nine in ten Year 1 teachers said the phonics checks did not tell them anything new about the reading ability of their pupils; 86% said they should not continue, even many who had been open-minded before administering it. Nine in ten had practised reading made-up (pseudo) words and many felt under pressure to teach synthetic phonics immediately prior to the test. Good readers who had not met the criterion might have their reading materials limited on the basis of DfE recommendations and were required to re-sit the check.

Furthermore why offer £10 million for a literacy catch up programme for disadvantaged pupils who are behind in reading and writing, but only at the end of their primary school, while offering only match-funding for more commercial synthetic phonics materials and courses for children designated failures by the phonics check? It is conceivable that a different approach might be appropriate for at least some of these children, while some of the younger children who failed might have matured sufficiently to pass the test a year on without the use of further phonics materials.

While the results for individual schools were not made widely available they are online for Ofsted to consult. What is disturbing is not that fact so much as the detailed analysis for individual schools with percentages compared with national figures, often based on very small numbers. For example in one school where there were only 12 children within one category and only 2 reached the required/expected standard there is a column listing that as 17% compared to the national percentage of 50%.

On the curriculum: A National Curriculum Review was undertaken and when the draft English Key Stage 1 and 2 recommendations (for the primary schools) were published, The United Kingdom Literacy Association responded with positive comments on some recommendations, but expressed concern at a number of aspects:

- the focus on phonics, not just as one of a range of strategies;
- the recommendation that the early reading will be from 'phonetically plausible texts';
- the effects on fluent readers;
- lack of reference to home literacy practices;
- lack of reference to critical literacy or technologies.

To quote: 'the soul has been taken out of the subject'.

On training: The dictates from DfE are not only having a major impact on practice in schools, removing the freedom of practitioners to adopt the approaches they think appropriate for their individual children. The recommendations by Ofsted (the inspection body in England) lay emphasis on the importance of checking that these edicts are followed in all schools, and in training institutions. HMCI Sir Michael Wilshaw, stated that

> 'Ofsted will sharpen its focus on phonics in routine inspections of all initial teacher education provision – primary, secondary and Further Education. Ofsted will also start a series of unannounced inspections solely on the training of phonics teaching in providers of primary initial teacher education.' (*Education*, online No 461 16 March 2012)

DfE commissioned the National Foundation for Educational Research to undertake an evaluation to assess whether the screening check is meeting the objectives set out by the Government. The research is funded from 2012-15. In chapter 7 the findings of the first two interim reports are considered. The final report is not due until May 2015.

Note: The report of EU High Level Group of Experts on Literacy, (ec.europe.eu/education/literacy/resources/final-report), published that same year, in September 2012, carries a very different message:

Its recommendations for the primary school years include:

establish specialist reading teachers and higher qualifications for all primary teachers;

ensure that all newly qualified teachers obtain a master's degree, with competences in, for example critical evaluation of literacy research and new instructional methods;

tailor instruction to student language diversity and engaging parents in their children's reading and writing work at school. (91)

Chapter 5

The Phonics Check: three years on

There have been some changes in the phonics check in 2014. For the guidance notes for administration of the check in 2014, published in February 2014, see www.education.gov.uk/ks1.

Background

In June 2012 the phonics check was administered to all Year 1 children in state funded schools in England for the first time. In June 2013 a similar test was administered to all Year 1 children and to those in Year 2 who had failed to achieve the pass mark of 32 out of 40 the previous year or to whom it had not been administered. A few changes were made for 2014 according to the Administrators' Guide for 2014, including a decision not to reveal the threshold mark in advance as in the previous two years. However, the pass mark was published online on 30 June, a few days after the testing was completed. Schools needed to know it to enable them to decide whether a child had passed or failed and to complete their returns, as pass/fail is still the reported information. No explanation was given for this decision. It does deal with concerns about the peak in percentages of children achieving 32, the threshold mark, in the two previous years. However, it was interesting to discover that the threshold mark was indeed the same in 2014 with no explanation given for that decision. In view of this change, the legitimacy of comparing the results for 2014 with the two previous years must be questioned. Among other changes listed for 2014 is the inclusion of 'maintained nursery schools with registered children who will reach the age of six before the end of the school year'. It is also noted that 'children who were not assessed at all at the end of Year 1, as well as those who did not meet the standard at the end of Year 1, are now included in the phonics screening check retakes policy'. For a light touch assessment the security recommended to the schools is astonishingly rigorous as schools are advised to 'Conduct regular checks of the materials to ensure they have not been tampered with'! Yet again in 2014 the check has begun with 12 pseudo words. See *Check Administrators' Guide* on www.education.gov.uk/ks1.

A comparison of the results of the phonics checks in 2012 and 2013

Results of phonics check for 2013

The test for 2013 was similar to the previous year, again with the first twelve words pseudo words (with coloured illustrations). The pass mark again was 32 out of 40 and again the teachers were informed in advance that 32 is the pass mark. To quote:

> This mark was communicated to schools in advance of the screening check being administered so that schools could immediately put in place extra support for pupils who had not met the required standard.

The results for 2013 are to be found at: www.gov.uk/government/statistics-key-stage-1. The pattern is similar to 2012, but with 69% meeting the expected standard, an increase of 11% since 2012; as previously girls outperformed boys. The results for Year 2 are presented nationally by pupil characteristics and include a local authority summary. By the end of Year 2 in 2013 85% of pupils (typically aged 7) met the expected standard. This includes those who passed in Year 1 in 2012, those retaking the check in 2013 and any taking the test for the first time in 2013. This is claimed to represent an increase of 27 percentage points from 58%.

In 2013 I again requested information by date of birth as this was not in the published tables. The relevant figures for Year 1 children in 2013 are 75% for the oldest boys and 55% for the youngest, and 81% and 64% for the girls. Again one might question whether the younger children might by the following year have matured sufficiently to pass the test without further synthetic phonics. No reference has been made to this in DfE statements so far.

Yet again in 2013 there was a 'spike' at mark 32, known in advance to be the pass mark, with 1% of children scoring 31 and 7% scoring 32. I had drawn attention to this anomaly in the previous year's results. The findings from the first interim report from the NFER research commissioned by DfE are analysed in chapter 7; these only took account of the first year's testing. I had initially failed to note, a significant comment by NFER based on the 2012 results in Topic Note: 2012 Phonics Screening Check: research report May 2013, (L.Townley and D. Cotts) where they are more pointed in their interpretation of these results than I had been, referring to:

> a spike at the threshold of meeting the expected standard, *suggesting that pupils on the borderline may have been marked up.* [my italics].

> By removing pupils' scores around the spike and using regression techniques, it is estimated that 46% of pupils would meet the expected standard if there was not a spike at the borderline' (28). [that is instead of 58%].

Since the administration of the check was similar in 2013, with the pass mark known in advance, it seems likely that yet again the numbers of pupils passing the check have been over estimated. There may also be differences between schools, or markers, in the extent to which borderline pupils have been marked up. This makes the whole exercise even more questionable. Were the pass mark not to be divulged in advance this effect might be minimised; however, it would no longer be possible to compare results from one year to the next. In the light of comments such as this I was interested to note that the threshold mark was not in 2014 to be revealed in advance.

Results of the 2014 phonics check

The Press Release from gov.uk claims on the basis of the results of the 2014 phonics check: '100,000 more pupils on track to succeed in reading via phonics'. This claim is backed in headings in various daily papers:

'Rise in children passing literacy benchmarks as phonics method pays off' (*The Guardian*, 25.9.14)

'Pupils doing better on phonics tests year in year' (*The Independent* 25.9.14)

The Statistical First Release from the Department for Education on 25.9.14 states that there has been an increase in Year 1 pupils passing the test from 58% in 2012, to 69% in 2013 and 74% in 2014, and that 88% of pupils met the expected standard by the end of Year 2. This includes those retaking the test or taking it for the first time in 2014. It is also stated that within the various groupings the proportions achieving the expected standard have increased within the last year. In a series of articles I considered these aspects in some detail. Here I will focus on the new evidence and the apparent impact on the curriculum. One aspect to which I drew attention was the large difference in percentage passing between the oldest and youngest pupils, both for boys and girls (Clark, M.M. 2014: 151). This evidence was not in the published tables last year, nor again in 2014. Yet it is a very significant finding as there is a full year's difference between the youngest and oldest children; indeed the youngest children might have matured enough to pass the following year without specific intervention programmes. The pass rate for the oldest boys was 65% in 2012 while for the youngest it was only 44%; for girls it was 72% and 51%. In view of the very detailed tables for other aspects it is a matter of surprise that there are again in 2014 no published tables with this information. I requested this, and found as expected, yet again a wide difference in percentage pass rate between the oldest and youngest children, with 82% of the oldest children passing and only 65% of the youngest. Thus 36% of the youngest boys and 29% of the youngest girls will be required to re-sit the check in 2015. Surely a statistic such as this should have been worthy of comment by DfE!

Value and validity of the check

The NFER research interim report has already raised issues about the costs and benefits of a one off test versus teachers being well trained to monitor children's progress (see chapter 7). There may be a faulty logic in a one-off pass/fail test, where the child reaches or fails to reach an arbitrary prescribed standard, a mark known to the teachers in advance; a test that is vastly expensive to develop and administer, which may over-estimate those at-risk; is not diagnostic and where there is no specific funding linked to the needs of individual children.

Costing the policy on synthetic phonics

It is disturbing how much money and time has been devoted by DfE to a detailed analysis of the results of this test which by most standards of test construction seems flawed, including a breakdown by types of schools and by local authorities. Furthermore detailed results for individual schools are available at RAISEonline, accessible to Ofsted as evidence for inspections, including percentages within the various categories (often based on very small numbers) then compared with national percentages.

It has yet to be established the effect this policy is having on the literacy experiences of young children in state schools in England. We need among other things to talk with the young children themselves, those who are failing and those who were already well on the way to becoming successful readers, to examine their opinions of the experience of the check, the extent to which it is colouring their views on literacy, and their access to a wide range of reading material. The views of the parents are also missing.

In chapter 6 the cost of the commercial phonics programmes and training courses schools have been encouraged to purchase with funding from DfE will be reported. The discussion there will be widened to include experiences in other countries, including US, Germany

Chapter 6

Whose Knowledge Counts: at what cost?

The first part of this chapter is based on an article in the *Education Journal* Issue 186, 2014: 13-16. The evidence for the second apart is from *Whose Knowledge Counts in Government Literacy Policies? Why expertise matters*, K. S. Goodman, R. C. Calfee and Y. M. Goodman (eds). 2014. New York: Routledge.

Background

In the previous chapter I questioned the cost of the commercial phonics programmes and training courses for teachers that schools were encouraged to purchase, with additional funding from DfE between September 2011 and October 2013. I noted that only selected programmes and training courses were available for such funding. The information I was able to secure under the Freedom of Information Act forms the first part of this chapter. In the second part of the chapter the discussion is widened to include information from The United States, France, Germany and developing countries where similar developments involving commercial programmes have taken place. This section draws on evidence from relevant parts of *Whose Knowledge Counts in Government Literacy Policies? Why expertise matters,* K. S. Goodman, R. C. Calfee and Y. M. Goodman (eds), 2014, New York: Routledge.

Part 1 Costing the synthetic phonics policy in England

Match-funding for commercial programmes and training courses on synthetic phonics

Over the period September 2011 to October 2013 DfE made match-funding available for schools that either purchased commercial materials or training courses from 'The Importance of Phonics' catalogue. The match-funding programme was managed for the government by a group of five organisations known as Pro5; an agreed commission was included in the catalogue sale price.

1. Over that period a total of £23,593,109 match-funding was provided for schools, approximately £22 million for materials and a further £1.3 million for training courses. As the schools could only claim up to 50% of their total expenditure on the phonics materials or training from match-funding, at least a similar amount was spent by schools. Furthermore this only covers expenditure during that period, and only on the materials on the list issued by the government.

2. The claim for the commercial programmes was approximately £19 million (excluding VAT), but it was possible to obtain a breakdown by programme for only Mainstream Programmes, accounting for about £11 million of the match-funding for programmes. The other categories were Supplementary Resources (£3.5 million), Supplementary Resources Decodable Readers (£3.7 million), Phonics Catch-up Schemes (£501,000) and Phonics Catch-up Supplementary Resources (£108,000). The three programmes receiving the largest amount of the £11 million were Read Write Inc. (over £4 million), Phonics Bug (nearly £4 million) and Floppy Phonics (approx. £3 million). Four other programmes were listed as receiving the rest of the money. It was stated in the response I had from DfE that, 'schools were free to choose which products and/or training to purchase from the Catalogue independently of the Government'.

3. A breakdown of those receiving the largest amounts within the training programme of approximately £1,095,733 showed that £546,614 went to Ruth Miskin Literacy Ltd, Sounds Write Ltd received £129,734 and Ann Foster Literacy £73,654. The remaining 27 providers listed received the rest of the money.

4. Over the period September 2011 to October 2013 when match-funding was available, it was claimed by 14,263 schools (233 for training only and 1697 for training and products).

Some other costs of the phonics check

I also asked further questions under the Freedom of Information Act concerning the cost of elements of the phonics check and about those involved in the development of the check. The answers to these are as follows for 2012 and 2013 taken together:

Distribution to schools including printing and collating £458,000

Guidance products £217,000

Item level data collection £176,000

Main data collection and production of the statistical first release £63,000

The total over the two years was noted as £914,000 plus £300,000 for the pilot survey. There would in addition be the cost of the NFER research commissioned by DfE. Not included in these figures are any of the additional costs to schools in administering the phonics check. These figures do not include any of the costs for the 2014 administration of the check.

Who were the experts consulted?

I asked for the names of those who were responsible for devising the phonics check. I was informed that as the answer to that question was 'already reasonably accessible' DfE were not required to provide it under the Freedom of Information Act. However, I was directed to: http://media.education.gov.uk/assets/files/pdf2/phonics%202011%20technical%20report.pdf.

That publication is the *Year 1 Phonics screening check Pilot 2011: Technical Report* of 131 pages. On page 11 of that it is stated that 'the pilot framework was initially developed in conjunction with four leading phonics experts: Jenny Chew; Ruth Miskin; Rhona Stainthorp and Morag Stuart'.

On page 18 the following experts are listed as involved in the independent review of the assessment framework: Alison Bailey, Bryan Byrne, Rhona Johnston, Maggie Snowling and Janet Vousden. I was informed that, 'The test was constructed by test development experts within STA following the pilot, including test development researchers and psychometricians, to meet the specification'.

From the detailed technical report I was not able to establish who was responsible for several of the aspects of the final check that I and others criticised. It was clear that the experts named supported the use of pseudo words. However, from this detailed report it is still not clear who decided:

- To make the first twelve words of the check all pseudo words;
- to inform the teachers in advance of the pass mark of 32 out of 40;
- to restrict the information made available (including to parents) to a pass/fail;
- for the lack of diagnostic information from the test, and
- that those who scored less than 32 retake the test the following year.

I wonder whether any of these decisions caused concern to any of the independent experts consulted for the pilot study.

I acknowledge the help I received from DfE and the detailed answers prepared for me under The Freedom of Information Act. Clearly these costs are only 'the tip of the iceberg' as they do not take account of materials or training courses purchased before or after the match-funding initiative and other costs to the schools in administering the phonics check. There will also have been costs to institutions involved in training teachers, as they are required to give synthetic phonics a high profile in their training courses. Many such institutions will have purchased commercial programmes and/or employed synthetic phonics experts as trainers on their courses.

Part II A wider perspective on the commercialisation of literacy policies

The book, *Whose Knowledge Counts in Government Literacy Policies? Why expertise matters* (Goodman *et al,* 2014) is in two parts: Part I The Political Realities and Part II Aspects of Literacy: the knowledge base. Part II explores many important aspects of literacy teaching, including the curriculum, text complexity, the role of children's literature, diversity in children's literature and the roles of writing teachers. Part I is the focus here, however, as it extends the discussion beyond what is happening in England and reveals similar concerns among professionals in other countries about who determines literacy policies and at what cost. The chapters in Part I of Goodman *et al* are as follows:

Kenneth Goodman: Whose Knowledge Counts? The pedagogy of the absurd (chapter 2);

Patrick Shannon: Re-reading poverty; reorienting educational policy (chapter 3);

Jacques Fijalkow: Neoliberal and Neoconservative literacy education policies in contemporary France (chapter 4);

Henrietta Dombey: Flying blind: government policy on the teaching of reading in England and research on effective literacy education (chapter 5);

Sue Ellis: Whose knowledge counts, for whom, in what circumstances? The ethical constraints on who decides (chapter 6);

Renate Valtin: About the dubious role of phonological awareness in the discussion of literacy policies (chapter 7).

As chapters 5 and 6 refer directly to policy in England and in Scotland I will consider these first. In chapter 5, Henrietta Dombey critiques the current coalition government policy on synthetic phonics in England discussed in the previous chapters. She places this in a wider context, stressing that we are enduring a policy that is likely to be counter-productive and that:

> The challenge for the future is to change this state of affairs, by persistently calling attention to research and practice in England, and to the experiences of our colleagues elsewhere in the world. (76)

Sue Ellis, in chapter 6, while contrasting the position in England with that in Scotland, stresses that:

> Literacy educators and researchers are finding themselves in an increasingly tangled political and legal landscape, where frameworks that help to locate what evidence really means in the context of complex interventions are extremely important. (90)

In chapter 4, Jacques Fijalkow points out that France has a highly centralised state system; programmes are decided in Paris and 'imposed throughout the country by means of an impressive array of training and control policies' (47). He deplores the fact that those whose knowledge should count does not also count.

> First, in spite of over 100 years of data collection and studies, research from the human and social sciences....... is not valued at all also, Second teachers' knowledge does not count either...... Clearly there is an irony that leaves an important question unanswered. How do people with knowledge that should count make themselves heard? (65)

In chapter 7, Renate Valtin cites similar concerns in Germany where politicians prefer the advice of those who offer simplistic solutions, ignoring the wealth of research available. On page 96, for example, she questions whether there is sufficient empirical evidence on phonological awareness for it to be regarded as the strongest predictor of learning written language in alphabetic orthographies, and on page 99, she stresses that: 'The task of segmenting words into sounds or phonemes is very difficult'. She expresses concern that preschool programmes in Germany disregard linguistic and educational knowledge about emergent literacy in school. Her final comment is:

> In kindergarten, time should be devoted to oral language development and to experiences with the *functions* of written language by providing a rich literacy environment. (106)

I have deliberately left until last the insights from chapter 2 by Kenneth Goodman. Although part of it concerns tracing the development of the programmes holding sway in The United States and how this power developed, there are also many important points of universal concern. He states that:

> While there are still major differences among researchers, the issues that should be the ones being debated are not the ones politicians and the press are highlighting. (23)

He refers to a small group of new neo-conservatives whose mission is to control the curriculum. The following quote seems to resonate well beyond The United States:

> Their strategy is to frame the campaign as reform of a failing educational system. They chose to attack reading methodology and write into law a simplistic phonics model as a key to making public education appear to be failing. They are responsible for the emphasis on testing, the labelling of schools, and the punishments, which are designed to lead to their privatization. (26)

Part of Goodman's chapter is devoted to the development and spread of a particular screening test DIBELS (Dynamic Indicators of Basic Early Learning Literacy Skill), a series of sub-tests each of which takes only one minute to administer. One sub-test is a test of the ability to sound out nonsense digraphs and trigraphs, the premise being that the best test of phonics is non-words where meaning doesn't get in the way of the phonics. However, Goodman claims that there is widespread agreement among reading authorities and psychometricians that DIBELS is a very bad test, yet the test is administered three times a year and those who fail are taught the skills of the test and retested. He notes a conflict of interest as the authors of that test were sitting on committees judging applications by states for funds, and making the adoption of the test a condition of approval for state funding. He discusses the effects of such tests on the curriculum and on teachers and reports a further worrying development. A similar test EGRA (early grade reading assessment) has been developed and translated into English, French, Spanish and several native languages. He claims that DIBELS showed little linguistic sophistication in its construction and that EGRA (early grade reading assessment) did not go beyond that. The story becomes even more disturbing, as not only was this test used in developing countries, but, in Senegal, according to Goodman, where the home language is French for only 2% of the pupils, they were tested in French!

Final comments

As may be seen from the information cited above England is not the only country where evidence from research is being ignored, simplistic tests are driving the curriculum, available resources for schools are being spent on commercial products linked to the tests and schools are being ranked on the basis of such tests. In the words of Fijalkow:

> 'How do people with knowledge that should count make themselves heard?'

Chapter 7

Research Evidence and the Phonics Check

The DfE commissioned the National Foundation for Educational Research (NFER) to undertake research over the period 2012-2015 to consider the impact of the check on the teaching of phonics in primary schools, on the wider literacy curriculum and on the standard of reading. The first research report was published by DfE in May 2013, *Evaluation of the Phonics Screening Check: first interim report* (M. Walker, S. Bartlett, H. Betts, M. Sainsbury and P. Mehta). Clearly by this stage only some aspects of the remit could be considered. In this chapter I will outline the findings so far and refer briefly to a research undertaken by Maggie Snowling and her colleagues unpublished at the time but reported in the media. In 2014 the Standards and Testing Agency published online for DfE, *Phonics screening check: 2013 post-administration technical report*. I will compare the findings of this report with the second interim report from NFER and also consider aspects for which there is still a lack of research evidence. The final NFER research report is not due to be published until May 2105; some of the remaining issues may be considered there.

The National Foundation for Educational Research first interim report

Background
The first interim report provides an overview of participating schools' phonics teaching practices and the emerging impact of the check. The evidence is based on case study interviews in 14 primary schools in June and July 2012, baseline surveys of 844 literacy coordinators and 940 Year 1 teachers in schools. The ways that teachers were prepared to administer the check and their confidence in administering it, the appropriateness of the

check for specific groups of pupils, and ways in which the mandatory check influenced the teaching of phonics in the schools are discussed in the report.

The Executive Summary

1. Most teachers prepared themselves for the administration of the check, and many watched the online video on scoring. About half the teachers also attended external training specifically on the check.

2. The median additional financial cost incurred by schools in supporting the introduction and administration of the check is stated in the summary as £400, but with wide variation, reported later in the report as varying from zero to £5,000. I suspect this is misleading, lacking details as to what individual respondents included or excluded in this figure, for example teacher time, supply cover etc. Furthermore, it does not appear to include purchase of commercial materials and training courses bought as a consequence of the implementation of the check. Any estimate of the cost effectiveness of the check must include the cost of designing this new check, of the pilot study, printing and distributing the check to all schools, the collation of the results, and the match-funding. See chapter 6, based on enquiries made by this author under the Freedom of Information Act.

3. The median additional time reported in supporting the introduction and administration of the check was 6 hours (with a range from zero to 40 hours and over ten hours of senior leader time). Here also one must wonder if these questions were differently interpreted by respondents.

4. Some benefits are acknowledged, 'including confirming the results of other assessments and placing an emphasis on phonics teaching'.

5. Year 1 teachers had mixed views on the standard of the check with slightly more suggesting it was too difficult.

6. Issues are raised about the suitability of the check for certain groups of pupils. This included not only pupils with special educational needs but also high ability pupils and those with English as an additional language.

7. Information on communication with parents was collected very shortly after the administration of the check, thus in most cases the respondents were only reporting how they intended to communicate the results to parents/carers rather than what they had actually done.

8. A third of the schools reported making changes to phonics teaching in anticipation of the check, increasing assessment, increasing time and starting to use phonics programmes more systematically. It had also stimulated discussion between Year 1 and Year 2 teachers.

9. Views on the value of the check seemed contradictory depending on the way questions were framed, since one of the key messages to emerge was that:

Many schools appear to believe that a phonics approach to teaching reading should be used alongside other methods.

However, it is less certain that this is an endorsement of the recommended approach of systematic synthetic phonics taught first and fast.

While nine out of ten literacy coordinators agree, at least to some extent that systematic teaching of phonics has value in the primary classroom ..., a similar proportion feel that 'a variety of different methods should be used to teach children to decode words'. (8)

It is open to debate why the staff interviewed have not fully endorsed the government's approach, whether from confusion or from conviction! (See also pages 19-20 and 23 in the report). It is commented that a third of survey respondents felt in some way that phonics has too high a priority in current education policy.

10. When questions were asked specifically about the check, rather than the value of phonics in the teaching of reading, attitudes were more varied. Many were negative, and a few positive, while others regarded it as 'broadly acceptable but unnecessary'. The researchers query whether respondents

may not have been fully aware of the rationale behind the introduction of the check. This does not appear to be explored further in this report.

Phonics teaching practices

This section explores current practices and changes made because of the phonics check. Most Year 1 and Year 2 teachers reported that phonics teaching took place daily and on average two hours per week. All case study schools also indicated a strong school focus on phonics, with daily phonics sessions for children from Foundation Stage through to at least Year 2 by most. The indication was that around 90 per cent of schools taught in discrete phonics sessions in Reception, Years 1 and 2, while for some it was integrated in other work. Letters and Sounds and Jolly Phonics are the most frequently mentioned core programmes. Almost half the respondents referred to their school being involved in externally provided training specifically focused on the teaching of phonics. Some schools had sent teaching assistants on such training as well as class teachers. This was often supplied by local authorities with some training supplied by commercial training providers, the most frequently mentioned being Read, Write Inc. (See chapter 6 here for nation-wide information on this aspect).

Given the level of training, external and in-house it is not surprising that most respondents thought their teachers were well prepared.

Results

The results in the schools where the Year 1 teachers completed the survey were comparable to the national average (61 per cent pass, 58 per cent nationally). Few pupils were 'disapplied' (usually at most one pupil), meaning they did not sit the check. In a few cases the testing was stopped when a child was beginning to struggle or becoming distressed.

Conclusions in the report

When asked directly, only two case-study schools said they could see some benefit to the check. The teachers had mixed views on the level of difficulty of the check and most teachers felt the check was not suitable for children with speech, language or communication needs and children with other learning difficulties. Reference was made by some to problems with pseudo words which distracted some of these children. In some cases the children struggled to communicate their answers clearly. The views were more mixed with regard to the appropriateness of the check for children with EAL. Here also problems with pseudo words are mentioned.

The survey found Year 1 teachers held mixed views concerning the suitability of the check for independent and fluent readers (40% regarded it as unsuitable and 22% very unsuitable). In only seven of fourteen case study schools had the parents/carers been notified in advance of the administration of the check. Further information will be required as to exactly in what form and in how much detail parents/carers have now been informed of the results, as not all schools would yet have provided this information by the time of this survey. Many suggested this information would form part of end of year written reports. Some teachers expressed concern at branding some children as failures; others had concerns about what to communicate as well as how.

Many interviewees reported no substantial changes to teaching but those who did mention changes indicated:

- A greater focus on pseudo words;
- more phonetic spelling tests rather than high frequency word;
- parental workshops on phonics;
- revision sessions in preparation for the check;
- an increase in the number of phonics sessions.

Key messages from the report

Among the key messages at the end of the report are the following:

- Many schools appear to believe that a phonics approach to teaching reading should be used alongside other methods.
- Most teachers are positive about the importance of phonics teaching.

It is less certain that this is an endorsement of the recommended approach of systematic synthetic phonics taught first and fast. While the researchers raise the possibility that there is widespread misunderstanding of the term, this is only one possible explanation.

Further comments

There seems to have been no discussion with the teachers of analytic versus the recommended synthetic phonics. There is surprisingly little reference to the age of the children, though some respondents did mention the younger children still only five years of age. Also surprisingly little reference is made to the inclusion of pseudo words in the check. It is to be hoped that issues such as these will be explored further in subsequent reports.

However, most teachers interviewed as part of the case-study visits to schools reported that, '*the check would have minimal, if any, impact on the standard of reading and writing in their school in the future*'. (7) Italics not in original.

Further research evidence: Phonics test 'accurate but unnecessary' (BBC News 5.6.13 online)

A research directed by Maggie Snowling of Oxford University criticises the phonics check on the basis that it has no prescribed course of action. The researchers measured pupils' scores in the phonics check against regular phonics checks and other standardised reading and spelling tests. They conclude that while the government test was accurate in identifying children who were struggling, it offered no information that teacher assessment did not already provide. They claim that the check tended to over-estimate the number of at-risk readers. I had the opportunity to study the unpublished report of this research. 'The phonics check: is it valid, sensitive and necessary', (F.J. Duff, S.E. Mengoni, A.M. Bailey, and M.J. Snowling). It should be noted that Maggie Snowling and Alison Bailey were among the five experts involved in the independent review of the assessment framework.

Phonics Screening Check: 2013 post-administration technical report:

In 2014 the Standards and Testing Agency published online for DfE, *Phonics screening check: 2013 post-administration technical report*. I will compare the findings of this report and the second interim report from NFER and also consider the aspects for which there is still a lack of evidence.

It is claimed that this document is aimed at a technical audience, but that it 'contains information that will be of interest to all stakeholders involved in the phonics screening check, including schools'. On page 5 it is stated that the technical report published in December 2012, concluded that:

Having examined all of the evidence gathered so far through the pilot and the live sample, the Department is satisfied that the phonics screening check is sufficiently valid for its defined purpose and has acceptable levels of reliability.

The explanation for this further report is that the policy decision to require Year 2 children who did not meet the expected Year 1 standard or were not tested to re-take the check means the DfE must provide assurance that it is sufficiently valid and reliable for this purpose. It is noted on page 21 that this year in year 1 and year 2 samples 'pseudo-words had a higher average facility than real words'. It is worth noting the comment on page 22 that:

> This could be an indication that there is now more emphasis in the classroom on decoding pseudo-words.

Is the above comment worrying? The above suggestion is supported by the latest NFER report. However, it should also be noted that there is more latitude in what is accepted as a correct pronunciation of the pseudo-words.

The final conclusion by DfE is that having examined the evidence so far:

it is satisfied that the phonics screening check is sufficiently valid for its defined purpose and has acceptable levels of reliability (page 23).

Phonics screening check evaluation: NFER second interim research report May 2014:

The second interim report of the NFER research funded by DfE, together with technical appendices (*Phonics Screening check evaluation: research report,* Walker, M, Bartlett, S *et al*) provides an overview of participating schools' phonics teaching practices and highlights any changes since 2012. It also explores the emerging impact of the check. The information is based on data collected from case study interviews with staff in 19 primary schools and mid-point surveys of 583 literacy coordinators and 625 year 1 teachers. The information was collected immediately following the administration of the check in June 2013. The final report is in May 2015.

Key findings

a) Teachers were positive about phonics as an approach to teaching reading

b) In the majority of schools other strategies alongside phonics were also supported

c) More than half of schools reported that they taught synthetic phonics 'first and fast

d) However, many teachers believe that a phonics approach should be used alongside other methods'

e) Most schools reported discrete phonics sessions for all children in reception,. Year 1 and year 2 and frequently in nursery

f) When asked about changes to phonics teaching since the previous year the most frequently reported change by both survey and case study schools was the introduction of pseudo-words.

Preparation for the check: Most teachers administering the test in the second year had done so the previous year. However, many year 1 teachers reported starting to teach pseudo words and carrying out practice sessions.

Suitability of the check: More than half the teachers thought the level of the check was 'about right'.

Impact of the check: It was reported that the check had stimulated a great deal of discussion. However, most teachers interviewed reported that the check would 'have minimal, if any, impact on the standard of reading and writing in their schools' (page 10). Most children who achieve level 2 in reading and writing at key stage 1 'have previously met the expected standard on the check at the end of year1, but there is a substantial minority (over a quarter) who have not' (page 10). However, to quote from page 10:

> Thus attainment in reading and writing more broadly appears unaffected by the schools' enthusiasm, or not, for systematic phonics and the check, and by their approach to the teaching of phonics.

Only about three in ten of the literacy coordinators agreed or agreed somewhat that the check was valuable to teachers. Furthermore many of the teachers interviewed in the case study schools thought the outcomes from the check told them nothing new. A matter of some concern should be the comments on page 12 that:

> The year groups most affected by the changes to phonics teaching were reported to be reception and year 1, with the single biggest change being the introduction of pseudo words and

> 'Familiarisation or practice session with pupils in preparation for the check...'

Next steps in the NFER research will include endpoint surveys and case studies; analysis of national pupil database data and a value for money.

In the recently published NFER report there is a great deal of data. It is hoped that the final report includes consideration of the following:

a) The extent to which the teachers do appreciate the difference between synthetic and analytic phonics.

b) Whether the teachers have accepted the government's demand for synthetic phonics 'first and fast only' in the early stages. So far the evidence is conflicting on this as the practice seems to contradict many of the statements.

c) The effect of the new emphasis on pseudo-words generated in many schools following the introduction of the phonics check. How do children, and parents, perceive the role of such words?

d) The effect on the curriculum of practice for the phonics check and on children's view of literacy.

e) An analysis of the children's perspective on the check and their attitude to literacy, including the effect on the reading materials offered to children who were already reading with understanding prior to the check.

f) A further analysis of the effect of this new emphasis on children whose mother tongue is not English, those with speech and language disorders and any who continue to fail to reach the required standard even by year 2.

Unresolved issues

- No clear rationale has been provided for identifying the mark of 32 as meeting what is referred to as the expected standard;

- no clear explanation has been given for the inclusion of pseudo words in the test;

- no analysis has been undertaken of the contribution of the pseudo words to the final scores, yet more latitude is permitted in pronunciation of pseudo words than the real words;

- the evidence of a spike in percentage of children gaining a mark of 32 rather than 31 in the first two years of administration of the test, a pass mark known to the teachers in advance, raises serious questions about the validity of this test;

- the implications of not revealing the pass mark in advance in 2014;

- the reasons for selecting the same pass mark in 2014 as in the two previous years;
- the implications of a large difference in pass rate between the youngest and oldest children to which so far no reference has been made;
- the needs of those who failed to reach the arbitrary pass mark on this test which may not be met by a continuing focus on synthetic phonics.

These researches raise issues about the costs and benefits of a one off test versus further training for teachers to monitor children's progress. There may be a faulty logic in:

- a one-off pass/fail test, where the child reaches or fails to reach an arbitrary prescribed standard;
- one that is vastly expensive to develop and administer;
- that may over-estimate those at-risk;
- is not diagnostic and where there is no specific funding linked to the needs of individual children, other than commercial synthetic phonics programmes following the identification of the children.

The children's voices

Lacking so far is any assessment of the effects of these developments on young children's experiences of and attitudes towards literacy. How will this greater emphasis on phonics in the early stages, the isolated nature of much of their tuition in phonics, the new emphasis on pseudo words and the phonics check itself influence their understanding of the nature of literacy and attitude to reading? We need to interview the children and gain insight into their views, including those who passed the check, any who could read but failed the check, and those who were required to re-sit the following year. Finally, what messages are we giving parents on how to help their young children to become literate and to value the written word?

Chapter 8

The Languages of Literacy: a postscript

See *Learning to be Literate* (Clark, 2014: chapter 21) for a more detailed discussion of this topic with examples.

There is surprisingly little research information on the difference in complexity in learning to read in languages where there is a more or less regular relationship between the sounds and spelling of words, or of learning to read in a language that is not your first language. Yet, it is increasingly common for children to learn to read in more than one language, and is estimated that currently at least half the world's children learn to read in their second language (Deacon and Cain, 2011). Furthermore, figures released following a question in the House of Lords on 3 March 2014, revealed that by January 2013 19 per cent of pupils starting school in England in Year 1 had English as an additional language. (*Education Journal*, 2014, Issue 193: 23) The effect of this on literacy learning has received little attention in the current debates on the curriculum and assessment, yet this percentage is likely to increase.

In a research entitled 'Foundation literacy acquisition in European orthographies', Seymour, Aro and Erskine (2003) studied the foundations of literacy in a number of European countries with more or less regular spelling. This revealed that in the majority of European countries children became accurate and fluent at the foundation level before the end of their first school year. The exceptions were those learning to read in Portuguese, Danish, and particularly in English. These findings did not appear to be related to the age of starting school. Thus, differential problems of learning to read in more or less orthographically regular languages, such as English, should be acknowledged.

The development of written language

People have tried to record words in some form throughout history; amazingly varied ways have been used for written communication. Some representations are closer to what we regard as drawing, with a direct association between the features of the object and the written representation. Written communication may take a variety of forms within different cultures and has changed greatly over the years. There may be differences in the way shapes follow each other on the page in written language, from left to right, from right to left, from top to bottom, or alternating (Balmuth, 1982).

The use of spaces to represent meaningful groups of sounds is a convention we adopt in some written languages. Those of us who can read tend to believe that speech also is in the form of words, with a pause representing word boundaries. There are no such gaps in the flow of speech; this may be one reason that we find it difficult to grasp the flow of meaning in speech in a language with which we are not familiar. We may not have sufficient awareness of the probabilities of particular structures within words, word endings and sequences of words, in languages with which we are unfamiliar, to enable us to split the flow of sounds into meaningful units.

It is a convention in alphabetic languages that there is a relationship between the approximate length of a written word and the time it takes to say it. The relationship between sound and symbol might have been otherwise, and is so in non-alphabetic languages. In *The Roots of Phonics: a historical introduction* (Balmuth, 1982) Balmuth traces the history of writing systems in general, and the English writing system, spoken English and English spelling patterns.

Features of written English

To any literate adult the relationship between oral and written language may seem obvious. What else could the letters represent except the sounds of speech? What else could the series of letters with blanks in between represent except the words we speak? However, young children and illiterate adults may not appreciate this and may be interpreting the writing they see in consistent but erroneous ways. They may not appreciate the functions of letters, words, numbers and punctuation. The language of our instruction may add to this confusion. When children come to learn to read, they have to learn to observe new features in order to discriminate letters of the alphabet and words. In addition they have to understand the language used to describe letters, numbers, words and punctuation.

Orthographies and Literacy

A valuable source of information on the impact of different orthographies on learning to be literate is the *Handbook of Orthography and Literacy* (Malatesha Joshi and Aaron, 2013). Two chapters are particularly relevant to the present discussion, chapter 27, 'The theoretic framework for beginning reading in different orthographies' is by Seymour. He points out that:

> Languages differ in their phonological and morphological structures, and these aspects may influence the way in which literacy is acquired. Equally, the languages have different writing systems (orthographies) that vary in the way in which speech and meaning are represented and, indeed in the consistency and logic of the relationship. (Seymour, 2013: 441-442).

He cites Chinese and Japanese, Hebrew and Arabic in one group, and alphabetic scripts in which the letters represent the vowel and consonant phonemes in another. These latter he divides into shallow orthographies in which the relationship is coherent and consistent (such as Finnish) and deep orthographies 'in which the correspondences are variable, inconsistent, sometimes arbitrary, and subject to lexical and morphological influences (English for example)'. (442) He argues that in shallow orthographies 'it seems natural to teach reading by synthetic phonic methods 'by which letters are decoded to sounds and then combined to form larger units such as syllables'. (442) In deep alphabetic orthographies, such as English, he argues for a 'combined method by which children learn basic alphabetic decoding procedures and at the same time master a 'sight vocabulary' of familiar words' (442) In his concluding remarks he points out that age of starting school and method of teaching in part determine the course of literacy acquisition, but:

> aspects of syllable structure and variations in orthographic depth, may be crucial in determining how the structures are formed and the amount of learning necessary for successful progression through each phase. (461)

In chapter 28, 'Orthography, phonology and reading development: a cross-linguistic perspective', Goswami claims that:

> Children come to the task of learning to read with varying degrees of phonological awareness, and so reading acquisition is never a purely 'visual' task. However, as languages vary in their phonological structure and also in the consistency with which phonology is represented in orthography, cross-language differences in the development of certain aspects of lexical representation and in the development of phonological recoding strategies should be expected across orthographies. (Goswami, 2013: 463).

She states that it is simpler for children learning to read in consistent orthographies such as Italian, Spanish, Turkish, Greek and German and they seem to acquire reading at a faster rate than children learning to read in inconsistent orthographies such as English.

Endnote

It seemed important to highlight issues such as these identified by Seymour and Goswami, as they make the level of discussions in England around learning to read appear somewhat simplistic when they fail to take account of the complexity of English orthography.

It is to be hoped that the issues discussed here will raise the level of debate around literacy learning and show the relevance to both policy and practice of insights from research. When making policy decisions it is important to bear in mind the complexities of learning to be literate, in particular in a language such as English, with its deep orthography. So far this seems have received little attention.

References

Balmuth, M. (1982) *The Roots of Phonics: a historical introduction.* McGraw Hill. A new edition of this book was published in 2009 with forewords by Jeanne Chall and Marilyn Adams.

Deacon, H and Cain, K. (2011) 'What have we learnt from learning to read in more than one language?'. *Journal of Research in Reading*, 34 (1): 1-5.

Goswami, U. (2013) 'Orthography, phonology and reading development: a cross-linguistic perspective'. In *Handbook of Orthography and Literacy*, R. Malatesha Joshi and P .G. Aaron (eds). Chapter 28. New York: Routledge.

Malatesha Joshi, R and Aaron, P. G. (eds) (2013) *Handbook of Orthography and Literacy.* New York: Routledge.

Seymour, P. H. K. (2013) 'Theoretical framework for beginning reading in different orthographies'. In *Handbook of Orthography and Literacy*, R. Malatesha Joshi and P.G. Aaron (eds). Chapter 27. New York: Routledge.

Seymour, P. H. K., Aro, M. and Erskine, J. M. (2003) 'Foundation literacy acquisition in European orthographies', *British Journal of Psychology*. 94.